BLAZE
WITHOUT BURNING

poems by

William May

Finishing Line Press
Georgetown, Kentucky

BLAZE
WITHOUT BURNING

ACKNOWLEDGMENTS

This chapbook would not exist without the generous support of Freesia
McKee, who was an integral partner in revising and assembling the work
contained in this volume. I would also be remiss if I did not mention
Marcus Slease for reading and commenting on earlier versions of this work.

Thanks to my mother for her steadfast support and belief; to my brother,
Eugene, for his encouragement; to his wife, Caitlin, for her generous
enthusiasm; and to my late father Walter for understanding even
(especially) when he knew he could not understand.

Let me also offer my gratitude and appreciation to Kevin Pilkington,
Stuart Dischell, Stephen Kizlik, Meggie Dimitrova, Bill Westmoreland and
Denise Marsa.

For their generosity and assistance in securing rights to the "Untitled"
Richard Frank watercolor that provides the artwork on this edition's cover,
we gratefully acknowledge George Bolge, Tariq Gibran, and The Museum
of Art-DeLand for allowing us access to the Richard Frank Estate.

And an eternity of thanks to Melissa, for so much more than can be named.

Publisher: Leah Huete de Maines
Editor: Christen Kincaid
Cover Art: Frank Richard
Author Photo: Bill Westmorland
Cover Design: Elizabeth Maines McCleavy

Order online: www.finishinglinepress.com
also available on amazon.com

Author inquiries and mail orders:
Finishing Line Press
PO Box 1626
Georgetown, Kentucky 40324
USA

Contents

For Melissa

We Cannot Speak

The grasshopper
will not leave the car,
thinks our efforts
to rescue him
are danger,
so each time we move
he flees deeper
inside. How
much better
if we could let
this little one know
we mean to help,
but how is the insect
to know
and who can blame it
for distrusting
humans, knowing
our record.

Through Wilds

What is making me so afraid
today? It is a bright day,
beautiful: sunbeams,
fluffy white clouds, gentle
breezes, idyllic. So why
this dread flooding
my belly? Why am I
wishing only
to hide away? What
will be seen in the light
that I wish would stay
hidden by darkness?

                    This cannot be the world,
                    it is too unfamiliar,
                    too changed, the distance
                    from the world I know
                    is too far It cannot be,
                    I will not accept it,
                    though it does no good,
                    only makes it harder
                    to deal with things
                    as they have become.

If you want the truth,
I spent the first half
of the hike wondering
how much longer
until we arrived
wherever it was
we were going
and the rest
wondering when
we would get back home.

Tonight I Saw the Moon Again

You are the cloud
that covers the moon,
but I will be the wind,
the light, space
between land and sky,
I will be what surrounds
you. You will block
what can be seen, but
your screen cannot be
between us.

The Plot Needs a Center

I want to write it,
but I am not sure how
the story begins,
or how it ends either,
and of course the middle
is a blank. Really,
I am not even sure
whose story it is,
or who is in it,
or where or when
it should be set,
but I do have an idea
about a theme
or a possible theme,
well several possibilities,
depending on various
undetermined details,
but other than that
I am quite clear,
it is just a matter
of finding the time
to work on it.

What Is Released

I reached out and pulled
the flame from the air,

held it in my hand;
a moment, it seemed fine

as though it were possible
to touch the blaze

without burning. The heat
rested, the flame looked

at me, smiled. I shook
loose of it, but

that did not
free me alone.

I Knew It Was Not You

I knew when I picked up my phone
and heard only the sound of air,
muffled and distant voices

that you had not meant
to call, but still
I called you back

pretending it might be
a bad connection
instead of an accident, because

you are in Ohio and I miss you,
am glad for any opportunity
to hear your voice.

They Say This Is Your Year

The idea is: a blue bird
landing to perch upon
my shoulder signals
good luck,
but the talons
on my flesh
don't feel like fortune.

Care for Your Tools

It tore,
ripped, shred
up, accumulated holes,
the seams stretched,
disastrous, but
what is that
coming out
from those holes,

something has found
a way into this world
through what
has been torn asunder.

What I Cast Out

There is an echo
chasing me down,
             spitting my words
    back, always unseen,
                 it seems closer,
    louder. What will
    it do when it catches
             up? I am not sure,
    but I hear its yell,
                 my own warped voice,
         hear it saying what I
    once said myself.

There Is a Space for You

1

You want to join us
in here; to enter:
you must leave
truth behind,
outside this door.

Do not worry:
it has a small voice,
we have many
much louder
to replace it.

2

Let me enter
this place again
as I have before,
do not turn me away,
though I have changed,
is this not still
my home?
Are you not
always my family?

Gone

Sun, I am waiting for you
in the still dark, the almost
light haze before dawn.

You are near, but I cannot
see or feel you, yet,
beyond the faint bright

on the horizons edge.
I am cold handed, waiting
for the warmth of your day.

A Restless Night Continues

It has been too long
of a night,

years long,
the sun is due,

isn't it?
How long can

it be so dark,
and how much

darker before
first light?

Is something wrong
inside me tonight? I feel

a strangeness, but
I cannot say if it is in

my body or only
in the body in my mind.

I want to focus, I do,
but what am I to say?

Each time I am thinking
on this, that comes

sauntering through my mind
screaming, "made you look."

Interlude

A Fragment from A Dream:

You will vanish into the air
and I will join the water
and the birds will fly
without spreading their wings.

A Restless Night Continues

The way things are,
why stay here?

Consider the options,
driving away, taking up

residence on the beach,
collecting shells all day,

or disappearing
into the city,

get a job, build
a new life from the ground

up. There are still
hobos who hop trains,

a life on the rails,
the freedom of the unencumbered.

It appeals too,
of course it does, considering,

but no one is fooled. Dream of escape,
but in the morning, still you wake at home.

Gone

That is not the sky
I remember. It is
too dark, those are not
clouds. It is not

the sun, or not my sun,
the one I remember,
I do not know
what sun that is,

but it cannot be
the same one I have
always known, this world
cast in wrong light.

There Is A Space for You

1

He was so busy
seeking answers
he never considered
that he was asking
the wrong questions.

2

What I Cast Out

What steps should I be taking
to cross this river?
       I know there are rocks
    laid down beneath
              the surface,
  but knowing they are there
is not knowing
     where they are.

Care for Your Tools

You think the danger
is the sharpness
of the blade, but
ask anyone who uses
a knife, a chef,
a fisherman, anyone
who knows at all will say:

the dulled edge
is the one
most likely
to cut your hand.

They Say This Is Your Year

They built a world
for you, it is perfect,
just right in each way
you could want, just
right, with no problems
or difficulties, a good
life. But you know

better already,
do not want
the choiceless way,
simple certainty.
It is too hollow,
imperfection built
by good things overdone.

I Knew It Was Not You

I think someone must be here,
again and again, I think
that I hear someone,

though you are in Ohio
and the cat is dead. I am
alone here, but absence

keeps shuffling
about the empty rooms
while I try to work.

What Is Released

Let me begin
dropping the stones

from my hands,
the ones I have carried,

each picked up
off the ground,

a reminder of
catastrophe, my hands

are so sore
from carrying

them. I do not
remember how

to empty my hands
of them.

The Plot Needs A Center

If it is necessary, then yes,
I will be a point, a coordinate
upon the plane, but
at least promise I can be
centerpoint. I could not stand
to be an edge, let alone
the vertex of an angle,
nor could I take being
one of the infinite, near anonymous
constituents of a line. No,
I will be a point, but only
at the center, where
it is not clear
if everything is arriving
to meet or emerging
together to spread
across this unbounded field.

Tonight I Saw the Moon Again

Do not walk down that road on nights
when the moon is waning,
especially not when it is a sharp
slit, a bright sickle against dark sky.
On those nights, travel other roads, or walk
the other way, up from here along that road.
That way is fine, but you must not go down
this road then. It is best I not explain,
or you might be tempted, thinking
you can outsmart forces you do not understand.

Through Wilds

I am swimming
the waters to your shore.

     No boat came to bring me,
     but I needed to come

even if it meant
risking this journey

     alone across the waves
     with only my will to keep me afloat.

We Cannot Speak

I do not live
in the country
of my father:
since his death
I have watched
that nation vanish;
I cannot call this
place his country,
he died before
it changed, before...
What would my father
say or think
of this new place,
what warnings
would he give
to keep safe
amidst new dangers?

William May, a fourth-generation native of New York's Greenwich Village, dubbing himself a "Neurodiverse Language Wizard," began writing poetry when he was 9 years old while a student at The Stephen Gaynor School, a pioneer in special education. There he received individualized support, allowing him to thrive academically, and, eventually, enabling him to attend New York City's highly competitive Collegiate School as well as earning degrees from Sarah Lawrence College and the University of North Carolina's MFA program in creative writing.

William's earliest schooling as an individual with learning differences in a main-stream public school led to feelings of isolation and ineptitude. Subsequent triumphs, the result of receiving the help and support he needed, fueled his deep appreciation for language as a tool both for survival and for self-expression. These early struggles, beyond developing William's love for words, manifest in his natural empathy towards others, and an ease with being vulnerable in his work.

His work has appeared in *SoFloPoJo* (Issue 14, "I Heard They Broke Up"), *Chameleon Chimera: An Anthology of Florida Poets* ("Our Plan Did Not Go Well"), and *The Centifictionist*, where he published the microfictions "English" and "Locksmith". He's also a featured poet in the Yetzirah Poets database.

William's journey speaks to anyone who's ever struggled to find their voice. Today, he shares that voice through readings, newsletters, and his podcast, *Argh! Not Another Podcast About Book Publishing*, hoping to inspire others to turn their challenges into art. Find more of his work, links to publications, and social media contact information at *WilliamMayWrites.com*.

www.ingramcontent.com/pod-product-compliance
Lightning Source LLC
Chambersburg PA
CBHW022058080426
42734CB00009B/1405